POP PIANO SOLOS
27 HIT SONGS

2nd Edition

T0210370

ISBN 978-1-4950-5874-5

HAL•LEONARD®
CORPORATION
7777 W. BLUEMOUND RD. P.O. BOX 13819 MILWAUKEE, WI 53213

Visit Hal Leonard Online at
www.halleonard.com

CONTENTS

ANYTHING FOR YOU

Words and Music by
GLORIA ESTEFAN

DON'T KNOW WHY

Words and Music by
JESSE HARRIS

BEAUTIFUL

Words and Music by
LINDA PERRY

BLESS THE BROKEN ROAD

Words and Music by MARCUS HUMMON,
BOBBY BOYD and JEFF HANNA

Moderately, in 2

DUST IN THE WIND

Words and Music by
KERRY LIVGREN

EVERY BREATH YOU TAKE

Music and Lyrics by
STING

(Everything I Do)
I DO IT FOR YOU
from the Motion Picture ROBIN HOOD: PRINCE OF THIEVES

Words and Music by BRYAN ADAMS,
R.J. LANGE and MICHAEL KAMEN

Slowly, with expression

With pedal

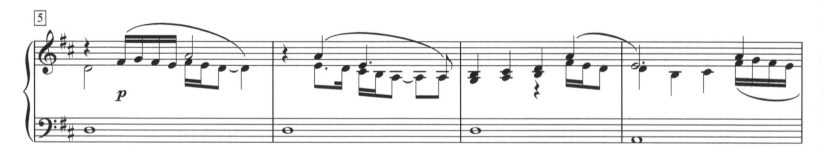

FALLIN'

Words and Music by
ALICIA KEYS

Repeat and improvise as desired

HELLO

Words and Music by ADELE ADKINS
and GREG KURSTIN

HERO

Words and Music by MARIAH CAREY
and WALTER AFANASIEFF

HOME

Words and Music by AMY FOSTER-GILLIES,
MICHAEL BUBLÉ and ALAN CHANG

I'M NOT THE ONLY ONE

Words and Music by SAM SMITH
and JAMES NAPIER

Soulful groove

I CAN SEE CLEARLY NOW

Words and Music by
JOHNNY NASH

With movement

I WILL REMEMBER YOU

Theme from THE BROTHERS McMULLEN

Words and Music by SARAH McLACHLAN,
SEAMUS EGAN and DAVE MERENDA

LANDSLIDE

Words and Music by
STEVIE NICKS

LET HER GO

Words and Music by
MICHAEL DAVID ROSENBERG

LISTEN TO YOUR HEART

Words and Music by PER GESSLE
and MATS PERSSON

100 YEARS

Words and Music by
JOHN ONDRASIK

TAKE A BOW

Words and Music by SHAFFER SMITH,
TOR ERIK HERMANSEN and MIKKEL ERIKSEN

CODA

YOU ARE NOT ALONE

Words and Music by
ROBERT KELLY

Moderately slow

THAT'S WHAT FRIENDS ARE FOR

Music by BURT BACHARACH
Words by CAROLE BAYER SAGER

A THOUSAND MILES

from LEGALLY BLONDE

Words and Music by
VANESSA CARLTON

THE WAY IT IS

Words and Music by
BRUCE HORNSBY

WONDERFUL TONIGHT

Words and Music by
ERIC CLAPTON

YOU ARE SO BEAUTIFUL

Words and Music by BILLY PRESTON
and BRUCE FISHER

Moderately slow, expressively

YOU RAISE ME UP

Words and Music by BRENDAN GRAHAM
and ROLF LOVLAND

YOUR SONG

Words and Music by ELTON JOHN
and BERNIE TAUPIN

YOUR FAVORITE MUSIC ARRANGED FOR PIANO SOLO

    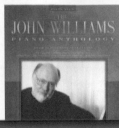 

ARTIST, COMPOSER, TV & MOVIE SONGBOOKS

Adele for Piano Solo – 3rd Edition
00820186..............................$19.99

The Beatles Piano Solo
00294023..............................$17.99

A Charlie Brown Christmas
00313176..............................$19.99

Paul Cardall – The Hymns Collection
00295925..............................$24.99

Coldplay for Piano Solo
00307637..............................$17.99

Selections from Final Fantasy
00148699..............................$19.99

Alexis Ffrench – The Sheet Music Collection
00345258..............................$19.99

Game of Thrones
00199166..............................$19.99

Hamilton
00354612..............................$19.99

Hillsong Worship Favorites
00303164..............................$14.99

How to Train Your Dragon
00138210..............................$22.99

Elton John Collection
00306040..............................$24.99

La La Land
00283691..............................$16.99

John Legend Collection
00233195..............................$17.99

Les Misérables
00290271..............................$22.99

Little Women
00338470..............................$19.99

Outlander: The Series
00254460..............................$19.99

The Peanuts® Illustrated Songbook
00313178..............................$29.99

Astor Piazzolla – Piano Collection
00285510..............................$19.99

Pirates of the Caribbean – Curse of the Black Pearl
00313256..............................$22.99

Pride & Prejudice
00123854..............................$17.99

Queen
00289784..............................$19.99

John Williams Anthology
00194555..............................$24.99

George Winston Piano Solos
00306822..............................$22.99

MIXED COLLECTIONS

Beautiful Piano Instrumentals
00149926..............................$19.99

Best Jazz Piano Solos Ever
00312079..............................$27.99

Big Book of Classical Music
00310508..............................$24.99

Big Book of Ragtime Piano
00311749..............................$22.99

Christmas Medleys
00350572..............................$16.99

Disney Medleys
00242588..............................$19.99

Disney Piano Solos
00313128..............................$17.99

Favorite Pop Piano Solos
00312523..............................$17.99

Great Piano Solos
00311273..............................$19.99

The Greatest Video Game Music
00201767..............................$19.99

Most Relaxing Songs
00233879..............................$19.99

Movie Themes Budget Book
00289137..............................$14.99

100 of the Most Beautiful Piano Solos Ever
00102787..............................$29.99

100 Movie Songs
00102804..............................$32.99

Peaceful Piano Solos
00286009..............................$19.99

Piano Solos for All Occasions
00310964..............................$24.99

Sunday Solos for Piano
00311272..............................$17.99

Top Hits for Piano Solo
00294635..............................$16.99

HAL•LEONARD®
View songlists online and order from your favorite music retailer at
halleonard.com

Prices, content, and availability subject to change without notice.

Disney characters and artwork TM & © 2021 Disney

0123
195